A. FRANK SMITH, JR. LIBRARY CENTER

W9-BWK-907

DATE DUE

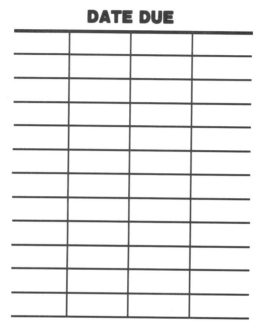

Demco No. 62-0549

WITHDRAWN

A helpful alphabet

of
friendly objects

poems by
JOHN UPDIKE

photographs by
DAVID UPDIKE

ALFRED A. KNOPF   NEW YORK

I would like to thank all the children who put up with
my photographing, without whom there would be no book.
Thank you, Annie, Anoff, Christopher, Hannah, Harold, Kai,
Katie, Kwame, Lorraine, Rosa, Sam, Trevor, Wesley, Waciuma.
— D. U.

THIS IS A BORZOI BOOK PUBLISHED BY ALFRED A. KNOPF, INC.

Text copyright © 1995 by John Updike
Photographs copyright © 1995 by David Updike
All rights reserved under International and Pan-American Copyright Conventions.
Published in the United States of America by Alfred A. Knopf, Inc., New York,
and simultaneously in Canada by Random House of Canada Limited, Toronto.
Distributed by Random House, Inc., New York.

Q-tips® is a registered trademark of Chesebrough-Pond's USA Co.

Library of Congress Cataloging-in-Publication Data

Updike, John.
A helpful alphabet of friendly objects / by John Updike ; photographs by David Updike.
p.   cm.
Summary: Poems and photographs present common objects
for each letter of the alphabet.
ISBN 0-679-84324-8 (trade) — ISBN 0-679-94324-2 (lib. bdg.)
1. English language—Alphabet—Juvenile poetry. 2. Children's poetry, American.
[1. Alphabet. 2. American poetry.] I. Updike, David, ill. II. Title.
PS3571.P4H45   1995
811'.54—dc20   93-29922

Book design by Ann Bobco

Manufactured in Singapore
10 9 8 7 6 5 4 3 2 1

C
811.5
UPIR

For Anoff, Kwame, Wesley, Trevor, and Kai

cousins all

apple

**An apple is red
or green
and ready to bite;
your teeth
and an apple's insides
are white.**

Aa

bird

**A bird has a beak,
a bright eye,
and wings.
In the sky,
it flies;
in the tree,
it sings.**

cat

A cat creeps along
and mews for food;
if you're no mouse,
a cat is good.
Its whiskers tingle,
its tail goes *swish;*
its little blue lips
smell blue, of fish.

Dd

dog

A dog
is jUmpier;
its fur
is **clumpi**er;
its tail
is **THUMP**ier;
but rarely
(compared to a cat)
is it **grumpier**.

Ee

eggs

**Made to be broken
and longer than wide,
eggs come in an eggcup,
or scrambled, or fried.**

flowers

Green plants get bored

with green;

they need to be seen

by bees

and put out flags

to catch bees' eyes.

Bees pollinize

these flowers with

their busy bodies

and dusty knees.

Gg

garbage can

Everything we cannot eat
gets put in it
to keep the kitchen neat.
Next day the garbage can
is put along the street
for the sweet garbage man.

hubcaps

**Along the curb you see them,
round and shiny; some
show you *you*, reflected,
stretched sideways like gum.**

Ii

icicles

They flash and shine beneath
the eaves like tiger teeth.
All silently, they grow
when starlike snow
falls on the warm house roof,
and melts and flows
to the roof's cold edge
and refreezes there,
getting longer in mid-air—
like a drip from a nose
that went and froze.

Jj

jam

**Jam spreads
on bread
and buns.
Jam runs
and slides and slips
and stains your lips.**

Kk

knot

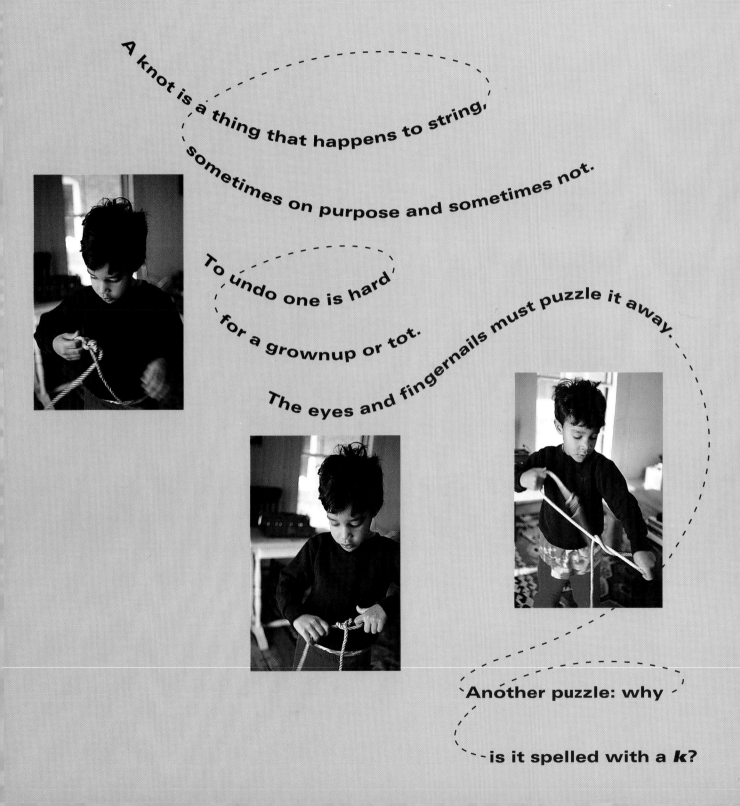

A knot is a thing that happens to string,

sometimes on purpose and sometimes not.

To undo one is hard

for a grownup or tot.

The eyes and fingernails must puzzle it away.

Another puzzle: why

is it spelled with a *k*?

lamp

Ll

A vase
for a base
and a papery shade
like a very big hat
for a little bright head
called a bulb: it's much
too hot to touch
and very very quick
to go out. *Click!*

mirror

Who's that in there?
He peeks, he grins,
his bright-eyed stare
(or hers) begins
to remind you of
that somebody who
is everywhere
where you are too.

nickel

Though bigger than a dime,
it buys but half as much
and less than one mere penny did
once upon a time.

oatmeal

As steaming mush

or tepid goo

gone stiff as paste

it's good for you;

you greet it when

you start the day

just as a horse

says hi to hay.

pie plate

**Aluminum, disposable,
it used to be of tin.
A pie needs something, after all,
to become pie-shaped in,
or else a pie would simply be
an apple jumble, or
a cherry mess, a custard blob,
and minces on the floor.**

Q-Tip

When Mr. Q invented it,
he didn't really mean
for Mom to poke it in your ears,
which are already clean.
He meant to make a tiny man,
a tiny cottonheaded man
with not one head but two
and not much body in between,
for you to feel much bigger than:
that was the funny, fuzzy plan
of Mr. Q.

Q q

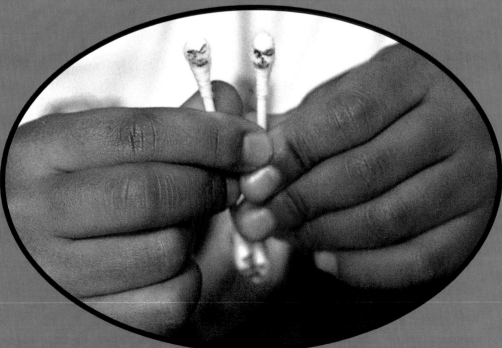

rabbit

At evening
when the grass is dewy
out hops the rabbit,
feeling chewy.
His ears stick up,
his eyes are pale,
and when he's scared,
he shows his tail.

shoes and socks

Shoes and socks, going on,
rumple, stick, and pinch.
Still, you wouldn't want
to walk an inch
barefoot on broken glass
or boiling tar.
In modern times, bare feet
don't carry people far.

Ss

toy

It's yours, and when

it breaks, you've lost

a friend.

You cry, but still

the broken toy

won't mend.

But then, so what?

A three-wheel car

still pushes, if you shove;

a one-eyed doll

still needs your love.

A toy is what we make

as well as break.

umbrella

It goes up
with a *pop;*
its curved ribs
keep you dry.
Its cloth roof folds
with a sigh
and the *snap*
of a little cloth strap.

Uu

vacuum cleaner

In goes dirt,
out comes noise!
Rumpling the rug
and scattering toys,
the nosy old hummer
bump-rubs every corner
so all those crumbs
of dust and fuzz vanish
into its hum.

window

A window isn't just

a sheet of glass

through which the trees

and sunsets pass.

It has a catch

and sill; it slides

up and down because

of clever ropes and weights

the window-maker hides.

Xx

xylophone

**Hammer it; you get
music instead of blame.
What a happy instrument!
What a funny name!**

you

You are an object,
yes, you are,
at least seen from outside.
Treat other objects
as if you were
inside them for a ride.
A cat has feelings,
this we know,
and maybe apples, too.
Umbrellas, maybe not,
but still, they ask
a careful touch from you.

zero

When the thermometer says zero,
it's very cold.
When you were age zero,
you weren't very old.
But you could cry, would learn to crawl,
and weren't a nobody at all.
Zero isn't just nothing, a hole to get lost in.
It's a round sign for marking
where things must begin.

Zz